Here
to He

4580

BUS
DRIVER

Hannah Phillips

Photography by Bobby Humphrey

W
FRANKLIN WATTS

Franklin Watts
Published in Great Britain in 2017 by the Watts Publishing Group

Credits
Series Editors: Hannah Phillips and Paul Humphrey
Series Designer: D. R. ink
Photographer: Bobby Humphrey
Produced for Franklin Watts by Discovery Books Ltd.

Dewey number: 388.3'22044
ISBN: 978 1 4451 3995 1

Printed in China

Franklin Watts
An imprint of
Hachette Children's Group
Part of the Watts Publishing Group
Carmelite House
50 Victoria Embankment
London EC4Y 0DZ

An Hachette UK company
www.hachette.co.uk

www.franklinwatts.co.uk

The publisher and packager would like to thank the following people for their help
and involvement with the book: Dr Mani, Mark Pritchard, Jo Erskine, Rose Thomas,
Padmini Mukundapriya and all other staff at the Bobblestock surgery in Hereford.
We would also like to thank the patients who took part for their cooperation.

Contents

I am a bus driver   4

Starting work   6

Safety checks   8

Ready to go   10

All aboard   12

On the road   14

More passengers   16

Time for lunch!   18

Cleaning and refuelling   20

Helping people   22

When you grow up... & Answers   23

Glossary & Index   24

Words in **bold** are in the glossary on page 24.

I am a bus driver

Hello, my name is Robert and I am a bus driver.

I work for National Express. Lots of people travel on my bus. I take them to and from work and school. People also use my bus to go to the shops or to visit friends.

Today I am driving this double-decker bus. It has seats on two levels.

Hello!

?

When did you last go on a bus? Where did you go?

The bus has big windows all around it.

There are six big wheels on this bus – two at the front and two **pairs** at the back. The engine is behind this cover at the back.

PULL TO OPEN

national express **West M** s

Starting work

I arrive at the bus **garage** at 8:30am.

First I go to the traffic office. This is where I find out what I am doing each day.

There are lots of notice boards with important information. I look at them to see what **shifts** I will be doing this week.

I also find out what **route** I will be driving today. Other drivers can see their shifts and routes on here too. These are called our 'duties'.

126-20	1405
59-11	1506
10-04	1517
6-10	1536
2-11	1537
529-11	1537
126-21	1547
255-19	1605
79-08	1617

? Why does Robert need to know this important information before getting on his bus?

Safety checks

I have to do some safety checks on the bus before I can go and pick up **passengers**.

Phil is an **engineer**. He checks the engine.

It all looks fine.

?

Why is it important to do safety checks before leaving?

I test the bells to make sure they are working. Passengers press these red buttons to ring a bell when they want to get off the bus.

The blue button is for passengers with a **physical disability**. They press it to tell me they need help getting off the bus.

I make sure that the doors and **ramp** are working so people can get on and off the bus safely.

Ready to go

I am nearly ready to go and pick up my first passengers. I sit here in the **cab**.

Just a few more things to do.

?

Why do you think the name and number of the route are on the front of the bus?

I press this button to make the sign on the front of the bus show the correct **destination** and route number.

I put the route
details into the
computer system.

This sends
information
back to the
office to show
them where I
will be driving.

All aboard

I stop at the **bus station** to pick up my first passengers. People are waiting for their buses. The timetables show people when their bus will arrive.

Timetable

Phone app

National Express also has an **app** so people can check bus information on their phones.

I open the doors for the passengers to get on.

These children are going to the shops with their mum and grandma.

They like to sit upstairs.

On the road

I drive carefully through the traffic in the town centre.

?

Why does Robert have to drive carefully in the town centre?

People are waiting at a **bus stop** for my bus to arrive. The sign tells them when my bus will reach the stop.

I pick them up and then we continue on our way.

I hear the bell ring so I stop the bus at the next bus stop.

A passenger holds onto a handgrip while she waits to get off the bus.

More passengers

I pick up more passengers. This lady is going to Stafford Street. I make sure I charge her the correct **fare**.

That will be £1.80 please.

She takes her ticket from the machine.

Someone is running for the bus. I wait for him to get on.

Now the bus is quite full.

? Have you ever had to run to catch a bus?

Time for lunch!

At 1:00pm I stop for a lunch break.
I chat with my friend Leroy.

Then I'm back in the bus
for the afternoon.

How is your day going, Leroy?

When I get back to the bus garage, I see that someone has left their bag on the bus.

How would you feel if you left something on a bus? What would you do?

I take it to our **lost property** office. It will be kept safe here until someone comes back for it.

Cleaning and refuelling

At the end of my shift I make sure the bus is clean and ready for tomorrow. I take the bus to the washer in the garage.

In the washer, the brushes spin around quickly to get the bus clean.

What do you think it would be like to be on a bus going through the washer? What sounds would you hear?

All ready for tomorrow.

Phil **refuels** the bus so it is ready for my shift tomorrow.

It is 5:00pm and time for me to go home now.

Helping people

I really enjoy my job as a bus driver. I like driving the bus to different places. Most of all, I enjoy helping people get to where they want to go.

I really like being a bus driver.

When you grow up...

If you would like to be a bus driver here are some simple tips and advice.

What kind of person are you?

- You are friendly and helpful
- You enjoy helping people get to places
- You are interested in vehicles and transport
- You are patient

How do you become a bus driver?

You must be a good driver and pass a special driving test.

You need to learn about roads and road safety.

Answers

P7. Robert needs to know this important information so he knows where he will be driving that day.

P8. It is important to do safety checks to make sure that the bus is safe to carry passengers.

P10. The name and number of the route are on the front of the bus so people can see which is their bus and where it is going.

P14. Robert has to drive carefully in the town centre because there is more traffic and there are more people about.

Were your answers the same as the ones in this book? Don't worry if they were different, sometimes there is more than one right answer. Talk about your answer with other people. Can you explain why you think your answer is right?

Glossary

app mobile phone software that can provide useful information

bus station the main station in a town or city where buses go to and from

bus stop places on a bus route where buses stop to pick up and drop off passengers

cab the area where the driver sits

destination a place that you are going to

engineer somebody who fixes and services mechanical parts of a bus

fare the cost of a journey on a bus

garage a place where buses are kept overnight

lost property an item that someone has accidentally left behind

pair a set of two things that are used together

passenger a person who travels on a bus

physical disability a condition that limits normal body movement or control

ramp the sloping surface that helps people get on and off a bus

refuel to fill a bus with more fuel

route the way a bus goes from one place to another

shifts the times that a bus driver is working

Index

apps 12
bells 9, 15
bus garage 6, 19, 20
bus station 12
bus stop 14, 15
cab 10
destination 10
disabilities 9
engine 5, 8
fares 16
fuel 21
lost property 19
lunch 18
National Express 4
ramp 9
routes 7, 10, 11
safety 8–9
shifts 7, 20, 21
tickets 16
timetables 12
traffic 14
traffic office 6, 11
washer 20
wheels 5